BURN

A LOVE LETTER TO

THE

OVERACHIEVING

SUCCESS

CORPORATE WOMEN

LIST

JAMESSINA

I dedicate this book to the men who raised me in corporate America. Thank you for your unwavering trust, guidance, and mentorship. To the strong women in my lineage who paved the way forward, you are inspiring and so loved. And to Keith, Richard and Summer – you are pure magic.

CONTENTS

Part 1

HOW WE GOT HERE

1
THE REASON

We were never fed diabolical lies, lies that insisted we could embrace both our biological purpose along with driving commerce and creating and earning. Instead, we are part of the revolution that began centuries ago and will continue on – for women to explore, embrace, choose, and cultivate all the parts of our feminine richness and potential. We possess the ability to literally create life and create ideas and things. We have an innate ability to morph easily between a variety of roles and bring immense value to the conversation, to the podium, to the industry, to our home. We wear many hats, all at once and separately, shapeshifting between them yet always at the ready to lead or follow in pursuit of life, love, power, money, growth, joy, unity, and inspiration.

With all this power that we hold, why is it that we feel depleted and a bit dimmer than we expected?

I wrote this book to heal my spirit, heal my body, heal my marriage, and ensure that I do not end up a lonely, rigid, wealthy, and successful old woman – with those I love enjoying life without me. I realized along the way that the light we crave is that which shines on our deepest and often suppressed emotions, and, if we allow it, could lead us to enlightenment. A defined and necessary shift that propels us back into life's desires, whether for ourselves, or for and with our family, our business, our community, the future.

Only we as women can comprehend the intricacy of our operating system, regenerating and self-healing itself with every experience. We unfold our lives like a dainty embroidered napkin, holding inside a warm, golden pastry just waiting to be enjoyed. Perhaps save some for later. Perhaps share a little with a friend. Perhaps indulge all at once. And if we don't enjoy it, try something different next time. Change is a part of life, and how empowering that we can manifest personal and professional joy that works for us, now in this stage of life, with a few modifications to how we operate, think, and feel.

We are each the spirit of our past, our present, and the possibility of our future. This life is the only one we know right now. Let's make it a good one.

Honor our achievements.
Embrace change.
Curate the future.
Impart knowledge.
Love the women we become with each new day behind us and another in front.

I see you.
I know you.
I love you.

2

THE OVERACHIEVING, CAREER-DRIVEN DILEMMA

She checked off all the boxes on the list she created at 19. The passionate woman on the precipice of becoming an adult, with big dreams and a long list to conquer. She stood on stage to receive her diploma with a smile and fervor to be unleashed and deliver on the promises she made to herself.

She was bright, and bold, and purposeful. She had a 15-point plan and the desire to achieve. She was glitter, and confidence, and poise. She had ambition and the yearning for a solid 401K and ascending while challenging the proverbial corporate ladder. She was unstoppable. And she did it.

We are the products of that passion and ambition. We are the result of hard work, building connections, elegant presentations, joint pursuits, business plans, and achieved quotas. We earn our keep and then some. We have built beautiful lives for ourselves and those we love, and perhaps created a few humans along the way. We are the culmination of boxes on a page, once a figure of our imaginations and now, checked off in feathery black ink with a flourish.

We were raised to be corporate women.

We were raised to pursue and achieve, celebrate our wins, and do it again. And again. And again.

We were raised to accelerate and enjoy achievement.

We have built and embraced an identity that has delivered on its promises.

The overachieving, career-driven woman.

This identity of the overachieving, career-driven woman has defined the course and has made possible the goodness and richness in our lives. It is the ultimate self-fulfilling prophecy influenced by our thoughts, actions, and behavior.

We now sit in this achievement. Perhaps from the bedside in a hotel room a time zone or three away from those we love. Perhaps on a porch with a breeze and the sweet scent of ligustrum blooming in the spring. Perhaps from an airplane, or a cafe, or the school pickup line. Yet, wherever we are, the weight of the years of pursuing achievement has crept in and left a residue on our reflections in the mirror.

The weight of achieving has us reaching for the space between our necks and shoulders several times each day or stirs us at the witching hour influenced by both our minds and the universe as we long for sleep. We cannot place the pain, the desire to run, but it feels as if a deep fissure in our beings has exposed a raw and undefined longing for something different – something different than what we said out loud so long ago. Something different than what we told the ones we love, or shared in the article, or defined and defended in the interview. The words have been cemented as our truth, but this undefined crack in our being has us torn between our spoken identity and something else.

Our spoken self prefers to assess and solve challenges to avoid any snag in the plans. This, though, has us cornered.

We checked the boxes; we've earned our keep. We have the trophies on the shelves of our personal, imaginary rooms of overachievement. We've built our lives the way we wanted with the requested results fulfilled.

Up until now.

The overachieving, showstopping, career-driven woman has reached a moment of realization that the plan, now in its prime, is no longer fulfilling, resulting in an emotional rupture in our sentient selves that feels as though we are splitting in two.

While we desperately aim to correct this glitch, the ache is unplaceable and leaves us unsettled. Questioning our past and our future becomes a bedtime ritual that doesn't yield the results we are looking for. We turn to what we do best: solving a challenge. We ask ourselves how can I fix this? But no answer is returned. Instead, we are faced with more questions.

Do I have too much?

Am I making an impact?

Am I happy?

What do I need?

One answer that is offered is true: *know that you are at this juncture now BECAUSE you did everything right.*

3

THE INFLUENCE

The number of emergency room visits is no badge of honor. This last one felt like the first one. Doubled over, severe pain in my chest, the right side. Numbness in my arm and an inability to walk, with recurring thoughts of the attorney who held our family will in New York. My mother drove me this time; the last time I drove myself.

No collapsed lung, no irregularity of my heart. Blood test – fabulous. CAT scan – clear. I was hydrated, fit, sober. Just an hour before I had been at my dining room table with a room full of wonderful friends, enjoying affogato and playing charades. The severe, gripping pain happened at my highest, most relaxed point.

I slept until 1PM the next day, wasting a planned paid day off. When checking the results of the tests in the hospital app, it revealed the number of times I had been in the emergency room over the past five years.

2021

Stitches to the eyebrow from rushing in between meetings

2022

Severe panic attack, chest pain

2023

Chest pain, immobile

2024

This one

The revelation of everything is not okay swelled in my throat.

* * *

An incident – or string of incidents – of this magnitude need not be the moment of revelation.

Perhaps abruptly waking up at 2:45 am thinking about work responsibilities later that day.

Perhaps the 'frozen shoulder' that apparently women in their late 30s and 40s seem to be contracting of late.

Perhaps the snippy attitude in the morning towards our partners or children or sweet pup waiting to be let out.

Perhaps the desire to shake out tears during child's pose at our 5AM yoga class.

Perhaps the weight in our chest and desire to scream when reviewing the nine back-to-back meetings scheduled virtually at work.

Perhaps any of those, or other less than ordinary incidents, could have signaled that something isn't right.

We attempt to alleviate the symptoms of these incidents with expensive and holistic remedies resulting in short-lived relief, with some happiness sprinkled in. The calm is fleeting as we find ourselves back to 'how we've always done it', where sooner or later the flashing warning signs find us again. We listen, we make a list on how to improve, often followed by a new passion project, deep cleaning of the linen closet, booking a vacation, swearing off alcohol, red-eye flights and sugar, and register for the weekly deep stretch yoga class at 7:30PM on Tuesdays.

How did we get here? Did we allow it? Did we create it? Or is it a forgone conclusion based on the teachings of those within our sphere of influence who could not relate to what our true lived experience would eventually shape up to be based on the dichotomy of our roles later in life?

Throughout our youth, personal life, and professional endeavors up to this moment, our sphere of influence has made its impact. The Oxford Dictionary defines 'sphere of influence' as 'a country or area in which another country has power to affect developments although it has no formal authority.' As humans in our own unique lived experiences, our spheres of influence, despite no formal authority, have brought us to this very place in time and space and success. Unearthing these individuals points to the moments and humans in our lives that quite powerfully affected our development. And it could reveal the spheres of influence which we would like to hand pick as we move forward.

Gen-X women (born between 1965 and 1980), grew up self-reliant and independent, many within dual-income families, or products of divorce, and we as a collective are highly educated[1]. We were raised in the continuation of the women's movement, and we happily headed to universities, Park Avenue office towers, and corporate behemoths. Particularly when it comes to business and leadership, women from Gen X and earlier generations were most likely to be influenced professionally by men. In a survey I conducted with corporate female respondents over the age of 35, 80% of their managers in their careers were male, with 100% having a positive experience.

* * *

I grew up in a typical household in the 1980s. My parents were happily married; my father owned a construction company, and my mother was a self-proclaimed 'domestic engineer' (a fine title correction for the more commonly used 'stay at home mom'). I am the firstborn grandchild on both sides of the family and the eldest of my two siblings, each three years apart, and the only daughter. I have never taken being the first lightly. It was and is to me a great responsibility that I hold dear. Reflecting back, it is easy to pinpoint the exact periods of my life where my journey was inspired by others, charting its course based on the teachings and actions of my earliest spheres of influence.

---

1 https://www.pewtrusts.org/en/trend/archive/winter-2018/how-generation-x-could-change-the-american-dream

At the age of six, I wanted to be a princess, or Madonna. It was interchangeable. I sang 'Like a Virgin' at the top of my lungs on the front stoop, sashaying down our walkway in the suburbs.

At 11, I wanted to be an attorney. My grandfather was a successful entrepreneur who is still to this day the only man I know besides Chi Chi Rodríguez to be able to rock pink plaid Brooks Brothers pants and a mauve sweater. My grandfather would call the house and ask which car I'd like to be picked up in, I always requested the convertible. He would say, 'Look outside,' and there he would be, on one of the first car phones in the silver convertible Mercedes in front of my childhood home. My dashing grandfather told me when I was young that I should not climb trees as "boys don't date girls with skinned knees." He also told me I would make an incredible attorney, and business law was where the money was. I loved sitting in his maroon leather tufted chair in his office of floor-to-ceiling windows.

I loved dinner at his country club, sipping Shirly Temples and being the apple of his eye. His charm, his lifestyle, his accomplishments, and his bright smile have all profoundly inspired me. He passed away from a heart attack at 63 years of age in 1993. I was 12.

At 15, I wanted to be on the cover of Vogue until I joined DECA (Distributive Education Clubs of America), a class and after school program that competed in business competitions nationally. Our DECA advisor, Mr. Pucci, will go down in history for all of us Calhoun DECA students as an eccentric and impactful influence during high school. Mr. Pucci was a short man who wore brown cotton pants, black button downs, platform black shoes and 1960-style rimmed glasses. He kept his black hair puffy and coiffed. He had a great Queens, NY accent and always spoke with his hands.

Mr. Pucci provided his students with a highly curated experience in class and during competition weekends. He told me to "pull up my shoes", or in other words, wear longer skirts. (It was 1996 and BCBG was my go-to 'business' attire at the time). He would write a four-page letter after every competition with private jokes and specific learnings for each of us. I posted one of these letters on LinkedIn in 2023, commenting on his ability to engage us, guide us, and leave a lasting impression that to this day we harness when needed. In that specific letter he advised:

- Have great posture and eye contact.
- Calm down and focus on properly setting up – use your prep time.
- Stay healthy, be positive.
- You close, not your prospect.

The news of his passing years ago left a hole in each of his students. But it also made many of us dig back through our high school mementos and re-read every line of saved competition letters to relive his passion for ensuring that each of us have a personalized, successful, and meaningful experience in the world.

At 19, I wanted to work for the National Football League. As a third generation Dallas Cowboys fan, I'd spent my childhood Sundays during the season with my dad and brothers in our navy and silver jerseys cheering at the television while mom brought in snacks. That experience and a passion for the NFL brand inspired me. I went on to pursue a degree in marketing and supply chain management at Northeastern University in Boston. It was during my undergraduate studies that two men in my sphere of influence greatly impacted my journey.

My godfather, Owen, was a childhood best friend of my parents. He was handsome, jovial, and an empath. Without fail, he (his assistant) sent me presents on both my birthday and Christmas. He lived in Laguna Beach, California in a New England style 'cottage' on a cliff overlooking Victoria Beach and Catalina Island. I could keep the French doors open at night and listen to the ocean while I fell asleep in his guest room. He took great pride in my pursuit of marketing – he himself had worked in the discipline in the publishing industry. I would ask his advice often, and two distinct phrases stand out:

"In negotiations, don't speak first. Allow the other party to share their stance before you."

"I won't work for less than $1,000 a day."

While at Northeastern, I had the great fortune of happening upon Professor Michael Power when taking the course 'Introduction to Transportation'. Professor Power, ex-UPS corporate management, made the importance of getting something from point 'A' to point 'B' efficiently, securely, and for the least cost intriguing. So much so, that I chose to double major in Marketing and Supply Chain Management. (With the rise of the Internet and a global economy in the early 2000s, Transportation had changed to Logistics, which then landed as the current term Supply Chain Management.) Professor Power taught us about 6 Sigma, operating within a complex organizational structure, the social and economic impacts on the way individuals work, and how to bring people together by being transparent, decisive, and honest. He also had every student prepare and deliver a 30-second elevator speech to the class, ensuring a slew of 20-year-olds could elegantly express their objectives. He and I keep in touch to this day, and he fostered my passion for a phrase I coined years ago: 'creativity with efficiency'.

At 21, I wanted to be on the cover of Forbes, and I also began my career in the Youth Football Department of the NFL at 280 Park Avenue in New York City. The offices at that time started on the 12th floor and ended on the 17th, which we insiders called 'The Field of Dreams'. It was here that the Youth Football Department called home and was also where the commissioner's office was located. Picture a spiral floating glass staircase, a large board room, and a receptionist area filled with Super Bowl trophies and championship rings. Commissioner Tagliabue was at the helm at the time and set a strategic initiative of serving 10 million youth by 2010. The Youth Football Department was in its prime, even having hosted Snoop Dogg (who created a non-profit youth football league in 2025, and claims that 12 NFL players have passed through his program) in a meeting with the Commissioner, Ridell, and USA Football to discuss helmet design improvement for our young athletes.

My first boss was Scott Lancaster, the Senior Director of Youth Football, who taught me how to operate in 'the real world' and provided life and work lessons that I return to quite often, even after 22 years. A few weeks into my role, I had an idea and walked to his office door to share it with him, where he was sitting quietly, pen in hand with a notepad. I began with a bubbly, "Scott, I have the best idea for the upcoming NFL Flag event, and I'd love to brainstorm with you…"

He looked up at me standing in the threshold of his office and said, "I am busy. If you cannot tell me what your objective is quickly, please schedule time with me instead." Ah, that response shook 22-year-old me, yet back at my desk I crafted a memo that identified the problem, a possible solution, and the requirements needed to bring it to life. Scott made me feel valued even with my earliest contributions, made space for my ideas, and later trusted in me to develop, curate, and manage the first Youth Football Symposium, hosted at the Miami Dolphins training facility, resulting in 90% of the franchises sending youth football or community relations representation to engage in two days of sessions, breakouts, and collaborative conversations on how to grow the sport regionally at the youth level. He showed me the power of uniting on a mission, engaging clients, correcting the misses, and celebrating the successes as a team.

Later in my career, my General Manager looked me straight in the eyes and remarked, "Don't ever hold back your ideas. Stop choosing your words. I want to hear what you have to say because I value you."

In my late thirties, I reported to a Senior Vice President in the enterprise technology industry who gave me a $25,000 salary increase, equity in the company, and a new title without me asking for it. He also was the one who landed me my next position after I resigned, which yielded a 54% increase in my annual earnings within four years.

These specific spheres of influence, entirely male, have had the greatest impact on my career development, learnings, and earnings. These men provided me with a toolbox of examples and insights on navigating corporate America – which I very much wanted to be a part of and succeed in. My perfect day then consisted of a pencil skirt and white button down with a popped collar, striding off the subway and onto Park Avenue into a glistening glass tower of success.

The pursuit of my plan, living it, breathing it, and seeing it in action fueled me. I consistently reaped the fruits of my labor and was always willing to take the early train, attend the late events, author the plan, travel to headquarters twice a month, 'man' the weeklong events across the country or on another continent. I worked long hours when necessary, sometimes coming home for a family dinner and then heading back out to events or meetings after kissing the children goodnight. I held a real estate license for three years to earn extra income to cover home renovations, driving around prospective homebuyers on the weekends and on lunch breaks while seven months pregnant. I said yes to my career and earning over and over again, on a mission to provide and climb. In 1999, my then boyfriend remarked, "You are happier when you're working than you are when you're with me." He was right.

I was a shiny, happy, stiletto-wearing professional… until the night I woke up and rushed to tend to my two-year-old who had a fever. I sat her on the kitchen counter to get the medicine in the cabinet behind her and felt like I was about to short circuit. I looked her in the eyes and said, "Do not move."

And then, I fainted.

My husband found me moments later on the kitchen floor resulting in an ambulance ride and stitches.

It was 2011, and it was my first stress induced event.

4
THE OPPORTUNITY COST

The irony of a curated career and operating as we always have is the desire for the peaks to continue while they wreak havoc on our physical and mental health. As stress creeps into the crevices of our physical, mental, emotional and career corners, the default is to push harder, work harder, do more, be more, pause less, avoid conflict, and be rewarded. Burnt out and depleted, we show up 100% with our game face, attend everything, plan it all, and as a last-ditch effort either work through the resulting physical pain and continue onward or eventually resign to take the much needed respite.

In turn, any time to dream, align, pause or evolve are pushed to the side as we tend to the bursting seams, ignoring our literal and figurative wounds while getting it done, left wondering how the time has passed and who this person is in the mirror. We fail to realize that the opportunity cost of our success may eventually cost us everything.

The opportunity cost is the potential benefit we miss because of a choice made.

As seasoned professionals, we make decisions often by reviewing the value of one choice over another. Leveraging our experience, data, team, and network, we identify the best path forward based on the projected value and how it will impact our end goal.

At work, the end goal is a predetermined target with an end date – month, quarter, year. This target is assessed at predetermined intervals and reassigned based on the achieved outcome, market trends, potential volatility, and experience. The team leverages their distinct expertise to build a plan, report on outcomes, and adjust accordingly over time. Sometimes, the plan is abandoned as the opportunity cost would be too high and to avoid not yielding the desired result. Amendments are made, and the pursuit continues.

Interestingly, we have not been conditioned to weigh our personal opportunity costs against the decisions we voluntarily, and sometimes hastily, make. Determined to check off all the boxes on our personal success list, choices were made over two-plus decades without the wherewithal to comprehend what it might cost us until later in our lives.

Every yes is a no to something else.

And we tend to say yes a lot. We see the potential gains in:

Yes, I will travel twice next month.

Yes, I accept the 30% increase in target.

Yes, I accept the promotion.

Yes, I will be class parent.

Yes, I will host.

Yes, I am available.

Yes.

It was easy to take it all on. I have thought and actually said out loud, "Do you know what I get done before 8am?" It's a defensive yet common statement amongst my female peers who run the division, department, company and home, knowing that they, too, have worked out, meditated, did a load of laundry, walked the dog, fed the children a protein rich, organic breakfast, made the bed, showered, packed lunches, and sent an email to colleagues overseas as smoothly and efficiently as if we were all 6 Sigma Certified. Or some version of that.

We can do it all. So, we do.

But we are bitter about it. We've been trained to perform at peak by our mentors, our male-dominated spheres of influence, but fail to acknowledge or blatantly ignore the trade-offs of a curated 'have it all' lifestyle combining a career and motherhood until:

- Physical pain
- Stress induced doctor visits
- Wasted time scrolling social media
- Lack of sleep
- Strained relationships with our partner
- Feeling lackluster and missing creative spark
- Avoiding social outings
- Resorting to mood enhancers
- Uncontrolled schedule

And it impacts our mood, our aura, our ability to connect, our libido, and kicks off a cycle of alienating those we love the most – those we do it all for.

But… We are the center of our life equation. Right now, that equation has us feeling depleted and in the negative. And as we know all too well, in order to turn a profit, we need to yield a positive.

How to get a better return on the investment we have already made for ourselves? Instead of weighing out all the choices we have made in the past, let's honor the decisions made by the fabulous women we were, as they have led us right here, to where we are today.

How could we have known that life would unfold the way it did? We were so engrossed in accomplishing the tasks, we rarely paused to reflect on the purpose of our pursuits. Let's not 'wish anything back'. Instead, look forward.

That deep fissure in our being? That unexplained ache? The growing pains along the way? This was the building cacophony announcing that the next stage is coming, suggesting we make preparations. Prepare for the completion of the original plan and the intended arrival of the experienced, intentional, creative woman we may become in this next stage of life.

* * *

I've built my life the way I wanted. But here I am, standing at the precipice of this next stage of my life – and I want to change it up. Shuffle the deck.

My eldest child is college-bound in six months. I want to travel to foreign cities and renovate the backyard. My car lease is ending.

All I can think about is change.

I want to harness this chance to change with powerful intention. I want the space to choose another direction. A reset. This feeling eats at me. My husband calls it my five-year itch: when I get bored and don't want to finish what I've started.

But what if we were not meant to finish everything, but rather leave it for the next chance traveler who sees and seizes the opportunity we left for them?

What if our opportunity is arriving, and this need to shift, this pull to reset puts us at a lower pay scale, no pay scale, unimaginable increase of pay scale, or in a completely different realm? What if it brings us calm, or exhilaration, or a deep, soul-fueling joy? Are we too bound by our accomplishments to take a chance?

What if all we've worked for is just that: an accomplishment. One of many. A trophy on the shelf of our personal room of overachieving. And now, we'd like to go back down the ladder, or up a completely different one. Add another trophy to the shelf for a different sport.

Job: 'A paid position of regular employment'

Career: 'An occupation undertaken for a significant period of a person's life and with opportunities for progress'

Passion: 'A strong and barely controllable calling'

Calling: 'A strong inner impulse toward a particular course of action, especially when accompanied by conviction of divine influence'

This calling has arrived. Perhaps it's a low hum in the background or a bold pounding in your chest. It will not be ignored; it is craving your attention. Even though it may be completely different or unique to what you've accomplished and said yes to in the past. A divine intervention is begging to be heard.

While every yes to something is a no to something else...

Every no is a yes to something else.

5

THE IDENTITY CRISIS

How can we even imagine or accept a 'something else'? As overachieving women, we are burnt out, depleted, fear for our health, and pained by not being able to be who we wish to be with and for those we love.

We never anticipated this new reality all those years ago. We never imagined that after creating all we ever wanted, we would never be able to quite settle in and enjoy it. Instead, we may end up – worst case scenario – wealthy and lonely or burnt out and depleted with the regret of missing out on the rewards from our labor, with strained relationships despite our great "success". What did we sacrifice that we will wish back? And, at the point of realization, when literal pain and deep concern for our health have made it clear, will it be irreversible?

* * *

I earned over a quarter of a million dollars last year. I own a home in a beautiful town near the ocean. I'm this close to Titanium status with Marriott. I lead awesome teams of humans who do great work. I am an executive mentor for the MBA program at the College of Charleston. And I support a charity I love deeply.

And a missed flight home had me rethinking every decision I've made over the past 25 years. Decisions that got me at gate A 115 at Bush International Airport, waiting for a Marriott shuttle only to return to that spot again 10 hours later.

I didn't want to cry over a missed flight. But I did.

I just wanted to wake up in my own bed, make my matcha, cook breakfast and pack lunch for my teens, do yoga, take a walk, fold laundry, weed the garden with my hands in the earth, have lunch with my husband, go to school sports games, have less business meetings and more dinner table conversations. Consistently.

I found myself craving home – literally and figuratively. Craving quiet. Craving an answer to this fucking ache in my being.

No battle cry, no mission. No pursuit. No game plan, no tribe. Not now. What I needed desperately was to breathe and create, quietly.

A spontaneous yoga class had my right hip, the one that had the chondroblastoma removed by radiation 20 years before, constantly throbbing. That class lit up parts of my body I hadn't cracked open in a while. Freeing, full breaths and sweat dripping from my brow and neck made me feel like a new person: someone who loved herself enough to leave their ego at the door and not pick it up until after class. Maybe even toss it away. How does that operating system perform?

Without the ego, we sit conflicted, reflective, and perhaps passionate about what is to come. We are in the prime of our lives yet experience a great divide in our being – a deep fissure splitting us in two. Is it dividing us between what we wanted and achieved and what we want next, the reality of becoming a new version of ourselves.

Letting light into this cracked façade, I feel both whole and crushed. This 'real me' is somewhere, and I'm starting to chip away at this extremely polished marble to find the edgy raw stone beneath. To shed some light, and some tears, on the fact that I am indeed evolving. This is not imposter syndrome; it's an identity crisis.

Interlude
A MOMENT

I have tended to crave silence during this past year. A quiet house, a made bed and tea on the porch at 5:30am. I want deep stretches and lemon water over late nights and champagne. I want less work hours and more focus on a few fruitful endeavors that will yield results faster, or compound over time. I want to know what I want and spend my precious time in pursuit of that.

At the moment, I'm too hardened at home. I'm irritable and not the fun, breathless girl I was 20 years ago. I'm thinking about insurance and investments and car payments and college and the smell in the garage and watering the lawn and getting around to writing my book. What podcast will inspire me, how to create passive income, etc. I feel distant, perhaps disengaged – and not very authentic.

My authentic self has been hard to catch. I think I pissed her off when I started trying to fit the mold of what a CEO was asking for rather than giving the eye of the tiger and amplifying my voice because I didn't agree or had questions about the strategy.

My authentic self is in hiding...she isn't gone. She's just scowling in a corner with her arms folded and big hair and bright eyes waiting to be invited back. Waiting for that sliver of a chance to jump back into my spirit and take charge. She knows how to operate at peak. She just flows.

She was once both a Peter Pan and a Tinker Bell – guided by the thrill and selfishness of youth, pursuing her every whim with a boastful and carefree attitude, alongside the idea that what she believed in must exist.

Goodness, I miss her. And when I realized she was gone I knew I needed to make every effort to welcome her back. However, enticing her to saunter back on in takes the courage to evolve.

Even the hardened rock will evolve in nature over time due to elemental factors such as heat, pressure, weathering or erosion, essentially changing its composition.

Accept the elemental and biological toll on our body, mind and spirit. Accept that our composition has changed. Accept that what we once believed in exists because we made it so, and it's time for a new thrill.

Part 2
WHERE
TO NEXT?

6

THE REALIZATION

The overachiever swings back and forth in a pendulum of intense frustration and great joy. The identity I've assumed the majority of each week for the majority of the last 20 years is the earner, provider, creator, matriarch, caregiver. And I have especially had a death grip on the reins of life since I added other humans to my unfolding life story. Starting with my partner.

In this death grip, everything is organized, manicured, folded, and on course. My course. Yet I have painfully realized that it is unsustainable. It doesn't allow for the 'what ifs' to creep in. It doesn't permit the surprise of great joys and the potential for life to happen for me and not because of me. It doesn't necessarily align with or allow the hopes and dreams and joys of my chosen person and my children. That death grip has unknowingly ONLY focused on how I believe things need to be done and has landed me a prescribed night guard and at times strained my relationship with my partner.

As overachieving, career driven women our success and sense of accomplishment are directly tied to our ability and organized efforts. While our demanding career roles can be challenging, we know that process, focus, and collaboration yields outcomes that can be attained, observed, scrutinized, and realigned. But what about when we stepped off the train, or the plane, or emerged from the driveway through our front door and into the space we shared with those we love? Into a home shared with another adult we chose who has their own ideas and dreams and way in the world? Into a home with small humans who don't yet have a plan, but somehow fit into ours? Into a place that has no working hours, but rather is always reliant on our last remaining shreds of patience, energy, spirit, heart, and boundless love to function?

There was a period of my life where the unruliness or stillness at home felt alien. Or I did – in it.

Where from Monday through Friday only three hours of daylight was spent with the humans I had selected or literally brought into the world. Where within the bounds of the weekends, creating as much joy and magic between 6PM Friday evening and bedtime on Sunday would be sliced into playdates, outings, sports, coffee on the porch, Legos, beach walks, backyard BBQs, drives, and maybe some silent space of my own. I found our family calendar bursting at the seams, and me working to add structure and a sense of accomplishment to my days off. And as a result, there are countless photographs without me in them or that I didn't take. My body was exhausted, my premenstrual syndrome created an unwelcome and looming week of frustration every 30 days, and my expectations of everyone to do things my way created a strain on the irreplaceable time with the loves of my life.

I realized at 38 years old that if I did not make a change, then the ones I was creating a life for and with would enjoy it without me.

I realized that true success is measured by the involuntary smile that crinkled my face, or the glow felt when replaying the day as I lay my head on the pillow, or the coexistence of the humans in my life whose energies are light, aligned, and effortless.

I realized it is the great joys, the surprises, the lives lived by the humans I adore that make me whole. They fill me up and brim over with bubbles keeping me in check that this life is a wondrous unknown and when I micromanage or over plan, I am holding back the floodgates of possibility. There is an idyllic flow that is possible when we loosen the grip and allow. I didn't know, then, how to achieve it.

* * *

For decades we focused on providing and achieving. For as long as we can remember, we were heads down and focused, permitting joy and wonder between the allotted 5PM and 10PM weekdays, on weekends and during planned vacation – if we took that at all. We are at the point where we have been shaken awake only to finally understand that we are not alone, that our female peers and sweet girlfriends feel the same. So, we silently quit at work, still achieving but not really present, dreaming of a golden parachute. Or, we en masse just leave the workforce and start our own practices, dive into a completely different industry, or go all-in on early retirement.

Is 'silent quitting' and the 'great breakup' a foregone conclusion to the original issue of us not seeing those who resembled ourselves in leadership positions in the beginning of our careers?

We cannot lay blame to our predecessors as understandably these few women we worked for and those we looked up to, even those we were frustrated with, were busy fending for themselves as they unknowingly charted the course for those to follow in pursuit of advancement, higher and equal pay, and a say in how business is done all while tending to their personal and family lives in the shadows.

Doors were opened because of them, despite us still feeling burned that they may not have looked back and offered a hand up a ladder rung with them. Too busy fighting for their own positions and their seat at the table, and putting the pieces of the family, work, life puzzle together, as they too, had even fewer female role models by which to follow suit, nor the platforms or access or time to vocalize en masse.

Was it always a foregone conclusion that we too would find ourselves in this conundrum?

Few today, still, are the even-keeled women in executive roles with the power, ability, and platform to demand a company-wide culture that provides opportunities for co-existing as a multi-faceted, overachieving corporate woman. These women are out there. However, how do you follow suit with the larger-than-life female CEOs, COOs and SVPs who pop up in our feeds or on the cover of magazines sharing the 'secrets to successful mastery of life and work'? Is their full story ever really shared?

What is the secret we long to be told? And why have we waited so long to unearth the answer?

Beyond parity, or sexism, or ageism – it's the desire to say yes to 'something else' that has many of us 'silently quitting' or a not so sure member of the 'great breakup.' While we desperately wish to squeeze more juice from this life we've created – we instead push harder and double down on our commitments. For my generation, saying no to 'something else' – our passions, our children, our relationships – was the cost of doing business and achieving the office with a window.

This concept, however, is experiencing a great revelation. A revelation that continues with us, who aim to make 'the something else' the actual focal point of how we change the tide.

7

THE REVELATION

Generations of women have been silently splitting in two as they realized the original dream doesn't fit them anymore. We were raised to have it all, educated and thriving professionally while embracing our personal life with ease. Content while collaborating with our male counterparts, be fierce and feminine, elegant and enterprising. Shatter glass ceilings while negotiating and working alongside those whose signatures we need to keep climbing. Find love, create and sustain humans, tend to a home, and have friends.

And like it. Because you asked for it.

And be grateful. Because you asked for it.

Overachieving, career-driven women are nonstop and often on autopilot. Operating at peak is average. Giving everything our all is non-negotiable. Otherwise, we aren't doing enough. When we do relax, whether for a brief moment or a well-planned and prepared for vacation, we are still connected to the swollen wings of our life stage filled with our identities/hats we change into at the ready.

Despite being repeat offenders of ER visits or restless 3AM worries, why hasn't the great unlearning of the practices by which we continue to work and live sunk in yet? Where is the voice of this silent rebellion enlightening us on the path to joy, freedom, and passion for the life we have created and the one we have yet to live?

SHE IS ALIVE AND WELL. And, she hasn't backed down. In fact, she's been much louder of late, having to resort to physical pain for us to pay attention. She's been stirring in the background, offering an unanswered tug, requesting some stage time to be heard, seen, and discussed.

I am ready to listen now. Are you?

But, so as not to sound the political alarms and backlash (from both men and women), we hold back the desire to scream that we want more space to tend to our children and our homes and our ideas and our passions and our bodies and our spirits. We fear agreeing with the status quo, but did we miss out on fully experiencing/embracing motherhood or 'making a home' as we pursued our careers with a baby on our hip and a partner who did double duty? Did we do 'enough' in our careers to truly feel that we have something to show for the decision to commit to our craft? Dammit, we wanted and still want both: remain a brilliant, financial powerhouse to feed both our family and our personal endeavors, and go to yoga class, bake homemade cookies, grow an apothecary garden, and launch the next great idea, startup, or unicorn out of the ether. Owning up to the fact that we are sometimes sad and want to be more available, accessible, and crave calm.

And acknowledge and call out our inability to rely on anyone else.

Including our partners.

I have always relied on myself. I have always thought of what I contribute, what I do, what I earn. I happen to use the words 'I' and 'my' a lot. And it was only recently that I recognized and confronted that.

Because I am a part of a team. My husband of 19 years is a handsome, 6'2" rocker who owns a design company that he founded when our daughter was born in 2009. He wanted to have something of his own should his long-time position as Art Director for one of the largest music equipment retailers ever conclude. And it did when we decided to move to Charleston from New York in 2015. And that smart man resigned and brought his business along with us. When I travel for work, he does it all. When I resign, he holds down our fort. When I fall prey to my self-induced panic he looks me in the eye and says: "You don't have to do it all."

While it may have started with 'I', for over two decades it's been 'we.' We created a home, we created a family, we are planning our future.

However: 'I' have been on a mission for as long as 'I' can remember and enjoy my pat on my back from 'doing it all'. In confronting this normal, I noticed a part in my personal history during a particularly self-induced tough time during undergrad when I wanted to come home and work for the family business.

My mother looked me in the eye and said: "No. YOU are a corporate woman."

Enter the self-fulfilling prophecy. This term, coined by sociologist Robert K. Merton in 1948, describes a "false definition of the situation evoking a behavior which makes the originally false conception come true.[2]"

This phenomenon underscores the intricate combination of an individual's beliefs, actions, and the outcomes manifested. Whether by the individual themselves or those around them, the stage becomes set to achieve the proclamation throughout its pursuit en force over time.

Whether or not it was false, I adopted the identity and the pursuit of 'a corporate woman'. It framed my trajectory, forging a neural pathway and range of decisions, behaviors, and networks, over time narrowing in on achieving success. It was the driving force of how I operated.

---

2   Merton, 1968, p.477

My vision of success resembled a 10-15 year checklist:

- ✔ Get the degree, check
- ✔ Get the job, check
- ✔ Get married/find a partner, check
- ✔ Buy the house. Have the babies. Earn the promotion. Go on the vacation.
- ✔ Check, check, check, check.

The success list was the goal. And it is tied inexorably to my identity.

The interesting part about this success list is that it doesn't comprehend the life that is woven throughout it. And how can it, as it was created at 19, 20, 22 years of age? A can-do attitude, a passion for the pursuit, and a vision of a life tapestry woven with a career and motherhood was pure and potent, the dream of living in the duality of corporate superstar and modern mother.

My 20-year-old self, all knowing with passion fueling her veins, went after it all. And she nailed it.

My 35-year-old self fought tirelessly to be a corporate woman AND a partner/mother/ Pinterest worthy homeowner. She pushed the wear and tear aside with a board seat and founding her company's first women's organization. She racked up air miles and took vacations with the family, held 'Bagels and Barbie's' playdates on weekends and handcrafted Ninjago obstacle course birthdays. She wrote business plans, ironed linen napkins, was class mom and generated 2X pipeline YoY. She won awards, she was promoted.

My 40+ year old self looked around and said 'something's gotta give.' She swore off alcohol after the pandemic, listened to the Rich Roll podcast, joined a book club, and earned another promotion. She keeps Salon Pas in her travel bag for flights. She celebrates family milestones like drivers' licenses and graduations. She is still CEO of the household while leading a global team and accelerating pipeline close or managing divisions. She scrolls the social feeds and shares homesteading reels and hidden travel destinations in Portugal with her girlfriends. The ducklings in a baby pool on 10 green acres or the Swiss Alps have her daydreaming of someone else's life decisions. And she returns every weekday morning to her home office, an airport, the workplace with bright eyes and a smile. All while suppressing something.

She is living her original dream but has woken up.

We have woken up.

We have realized a few things.

The success list was achievable; we mastered the art of going after it. The life markers on our journeys were as we thought they'd be – worked for, celebrated, racked up, and doubled down upon as we progressed. Our spheres of influence taught us well, mission forward and forward thinking.

At this specific juncture in our lives, however, we realize our blatant disregard of an inner conflict producing signs over time that life may have been eased with some adjustments, some measures taken.

How could we possibly imagine the struggle we would now endure resulting from the vast differences between us and our spheres of influence when there was no one, or barely anyone, who resembled us at the peak of performance? Our male leadership rarely called out to tend to an ill child, arrived late after attending a primary school event, or felt deep guilt for choosing the business meeting over bedtime stories – or they just didn't speak about it. Our male leadership did not include us in the team bonding fishing, skiing or hunting trip – or it didn't even cross their minds to ask us. The men who brought us along for the ride, who taught us, who believed in us, who still champion us (even those who work for us) have an unspoken, subconscious expectation for us to deliver despite our responsibilities. So, we learned to choose our battles and chose to keep moving forward with no roadmap or influence other than the desire to have it all.

The much-needed guidance and wit of women with the lived experience of winning while wanting failed to materialize until much later in our lives – and most likely it is from ourselves and our female peers. We willingly impart this earned knowledge on younger versions of ourselves as mentors or organizers of women's groups in business enlightenment, highlighting that the success list is powerful, yet there is another guiding force for women that can provide a roadmap for achieving a life well lived.

This is the part where we acknowledge the inner conflict that has brought us together at this time, where we reflect on the staggering pile of moments of repressed creativity, unnecessary rigidity, self-doubt, and insufficient self-care. It's time to stop the stress-induced disrupted neuroplasticity[3] and design the next 5, 10, 20 years based on what we crave, who we love, and our desires as the well rooted, creative, knowing women that we are.

This is not a middle finger to the men who held our hands along the way. It's an acknowledgment of their support and guidance and our gratitude for bringing us along with them. It's also, finally, our enlightened understanding of the era in which we were raised in corporate America and our vast biological differences as women. *It's a thank you, we have it from here.*

---

3   https://www.psychologytoday.com/us/basics/
neuroplasticity#:~:text=The%20disruption%20of%20neuroplasticity%20
by,behaving%20or%20fear%2Dbased%20memories

8

IGNITE

Let's begin by assessing that success list. It's time to take inventory of what we have achieved and what we have yet to achieve – comparing the latter to the women we are today and the dreams we have now. Even in moments of awareness when our pencil hits the page to unearth our new or repressed pursuits, we may find our minds wandering, our names called, a text, a ping, a recollection of something we forgot to do that steals us away. And we get up, yet again, to take care of everything else while our spirits beg for our attention.

Because everything else is easy. Doing it all is easy. Exhausting, but easy. Success is easy. Taking charge is easy. Being this overachieving, fruitful, giving, commanding woman is easy. And in the wake of easy, we subconsciously wear our hard-earned identity like armor, this shield forged from decades of personal and professional accomplishments and accolades. It offers protection from the vulnerability of the unknown, allowing us to navigate the complex and demanding with purpose and security.

But armor, while strong, is confining. Beneath its weight it has been hard to adapt, to embrace the unfamiliar, to grow beyond what we know. Shedding this armor forces us to face our world unguarded, daring to redefine how we enter the unknown and willingly discover who we wish to be beyond the identities we have built.

The original plan – our roadmap to success – had our best interests in mind, then, likely forged between being a fledgling adult and 20-something. It was created by a version of ourselves who had the rest of her life ahead of her. It was drafted from a state of great conviction, wonder, dreams and shiny, unabated youthful fervor. It was drafted from a time and space where we were the prime responsibility of ourselves.

It was drafted when our stake in the ground had yet to be staked, and we looked up at the mountain of desired milestones with a sparkle in our eyes and pages of a career passport to be stamped.

What has been checked off is done and should be celebrated as a mile marker on our lives' journeys. What has yet to be accomplished on that list, however, is officially under review.

It's time to burn the success list and start over.

It is an act of liberation, a release of our own expectations that defined us for so long. As the flames consume the checked and unchecked boxes, we are free to release what no longer serves us.

Burn the success list. Set the laundry list of pursuits ablaze. Let the embers flit and settle as ash, nourishing what's yet to come, serving as fertile ground to plant seeds for our next era. One that is both rooted by our curated, accomplished past and boundless with the acceptance that we are strong, beautiful, multi-faceted women who are endlessly evolving.

9

THE INVITATION

It sounds like a radical idea, to set fire to a work of art, to shed an identity that we have chiseled into a masterpiece over time, one that has brought abundance in life and at work, yet has begun to tarnish and overheat, and requires immediate maintenance.

Despite our exhaustion and pent-up resentment, our dreams of achieving duality as executive, leader, mother, community citizen have been achieved. Our careers continue to trend up, our children are growing or grown, and the threshold of the next phase of feminine life lies ahead. We want more; we want it all. We also want some peace. Peace from the mundane, while permitting us space to put our Pinterest boards to action. Glamour and grit.

And we finally begin to understand that all this time, we had the option to make 'the something else' a priority, but we thought choosing 'the something else' might cost us our careers and our ability to leave our mark. The calling continues to tug at us.

The calling begs us to curate this beautiful life as we see fit, flowing through our experiences focused not just on doing, but living, authentically as whoever we are at this moment, seeking what fills us up no matter how busy, or accomplished, or quiet, we desire to be.

Burning the success list allows a moment for this great consideration.

* * *

For the past eight years, this very consideration provided me the pleasure of guest lecturing for the incoming cohort of the MBA program at the College of Charleston. The topic is 'career envisioning', and who better to speak on that than the girl whose career trajectory crossed several industries and didn't even know the current industry she is in (enterprise technology) existed 20 years ago? The purpose of my lecture is to have our future business leaders guiding their career decisions based on operating as their best selves, scheduling their musts, aligning with their core values, and seeking fulfillment.

This annual conversation holds the exact knowledge I wish had been shared with me repeatedly at 23, 27, 32, 38 years of age: that my best self isn't just a reflection of my career decisions, but rather my *life* decisions. And that anyone can continue to evolve, share their learnings, and pave the way for those after them.

An inspiration for this lecture is from a period of time when those delicious photographs and videos were captured of my children at two and four years old. I am not in those images – I didn't take them. I wasn't there. I was working. On weekends, on evenings, to amass any additional wealth and leg up I could for my family of four. This gainful enterprise was not to 'make ends meet' but rather a singular decision on my part to get ahead, to achieve more. Looking back with no regrets, while I appreciate my enterprising 29-year-old self, I would have loved to be present for the laughter and the energy in those lived memories shared with my three favorite humans.

This example I share with our future business leaders is the very idea that my personal success plan was never knowingly curated beyond its first iteration, that I had operated in pursuit of something I created at 19 years old and that became my default. While I may have weighed my options at those junctures, I chose the success list over 'the something else' many times.

Instead, I propose to these enterprising students, and now to you, a more fluid course of success that involves reflection, projection, and alignment with the acceptance of our evolution. Our life choices have impacted us in ways we never expected, as our original success plan has and will continue to change – so will we. This is an invitation to see what our spirit has to say about our next era. It's a rediscovery of ourselves through visualization, guided by our heart and past. From our deepest memories and moments of once fleeting emotions, we unearth an achievable vision of fulfillment that aligns with who we are now—not who we were when we first defined success. It's a chance to rewrite the narrative, moving away from the rigid checklist of accomplishments and toward a life that feels both expansive and deep. We are not abandoning ambition, rather redirecting our actions to honor and cultivate growth, value, and joy.

*　*　*

Has today been spent exactly as you wanted to spend it? Has the last week, or month, or year been what you envisioned it to be in your mind, your heart, your Passion Planner or notes app? The answer is most likely 'somewhat' or 'no', with the proverbial laundry list of work and life taking precedence along with both scheduled and impromptu drop offs, pick-ups, dinners, calls, flights, headaches, appointments that often land you in soft pants before 8pm.

Set your phone timer for 10 minutes and let's sink into these questions.

Take this moment to breathe fully from your belly to your forehead, inhaling and exhaling through your nose fully. Take three breaths to really settle into your delicious human body.

Think of a moment that you felt the proudest. What took place? Who were you with? Note every detail about this moment – the surroundings, the sounds, your emotions, the look on your face. Feel the pride dripping from your being, immerse yourself in it.

Take a moment to write it down in great detail.

Again, breathe fully from your belly to your forehead and think of a moment in your life when you felt absolute unbridled joy. What took place? Who were you with? Note every detail about this moment – the surroundings, the sounds, your emotions, the look on your face. Feel the joy beaming from your being, immerse yourself in it.

Take a moment to write it down in great detail.

When done, re-read your proudest moment. Pride is a sense of deep satisfaction and value, and on this day, that moment came to you as one where you honor yourself or another.

Leveraging that emotion….. Where in your life can that feeling be replicated? For example, during one of my visualization sessions my proudest moment was the first day I walked through the doors of 280 Park Avenue as an employee of the National Football League. Another was my first time abroad for work, stepping off a plane in Tokyo to meet with a prospect. In each of my moments, it was the symbolic crossing of a threshold of a new pursuit and the sense that my peers trust and value me created a sense of pride.

While it is natural to pursue this state of being in everyday work such as a presentation, a campaign launch, a work event – where can this deep sense of accomplishment and pride be experienced in your personal life? Where do you appreciate your tenacity, contribution of expertise or time, or attention to detail? Where does the sense of value of another's accomplishments or endeavors bring you great satisfaction? Write these down and acknowledge your tenacity, your journey, your earned place, or those of another.

Pride can give us goosebumps and offer a gentle pat on the back reminding us that 'we've done good.'

Now, re-read your most joyful memory. Joy is an innate, spontaneous emotion, and during this visualization, that moment warmed you up and filled you to the brim.

Leveraging that feeling... where in your life can that feeling be replicated? For example, a memory that most often finds itself into my joy visualization is an evening in 1994 with my brothers and parents at Jones Beach in Long Island, NY. We were boogie boarding off the beaten path stretch of beach by the dunes, with rough waves crashing and seafoam streaming through our hair, laughter filling the salty air. In this simple moment, the pure and youthful joy is unbridled. Another core memory that finds its way into this practice often is the evening my daughter was born. Alone in the hospital overnight, I return to the feeling of soaking her up all to myself, the perfectly pouted baby lips, the nestled comfort of her in my arms, and the awe and newness of life. In these moments, there is no other expectation but to simply be.

I encourage you to take the opportunity to recreate – or simply acknowledge – this state of being in everyday life. How does your moment of joy in this session resonate for you and where can you create and prioritize raw moments without the rigid confines of expectation?

Emotions drive action. Pride and joy brought into your everyday will create a stream of sensory emotion that fulfills your spirit. But who is the woman experiencing this fulfillment? Who is she, now? I invite you to reintroduce yourself to her. She may surprise you.

Visualize a mirror in front of you, your reflection staring back at YOU as your absolute best self. Soak her up with every one of your senses. What does she look like? What is she wearing? How is her hair done? What is the expression on her face? Where is she off to or where has she been? What is her body language? What is she exuding? Take a deep breath and feel this version of yourself deep in your spirit, take all of her in.

Write a description of the reflection of your best self in that mirror. Note as many details about what she embodied and represented.

This reflection is an open invitation to acknowledge and admire the highest sense of yourself. The magnificence of the best version of her is here for the taking at any moment.

She is, quite literally, you.

What in that reflection is available at this moment for you to embody? Perhaps unknitting your brow, sitting up straighter, shoulders back and relaxed, allowing a slight smile to grace your lips. Perhaps it's a change of location in your home or office or airport at this moment to make you feel a bit lighter or on purpose. Perhaps it's planning tomorrow, today. Perhaps it's a consideration to shift the way you speak or think to yourself in your head, remembering your eyes are the window to your soul and what do you wish to share with those who look you in the eye?

Perhaps it's a consideration of what, and who, is now. At 30, I still recognized the 'showstopping, career driven woman' with the power pose in the mirror. She was shiny and stressed, gripping the mission to provide and earn and become. Now at 40+, the reflection winks at me subtly, with her wiser, yearning eyes and noticeable lines from the decades of laughter, worry, passion, effort, living. She deserves a new acknowledgment, one that is unique to who I am now, what my heart and most sacral being is asking me to recognize.

Who is that very changed woman in the mirror?

Not who she is on paper, or who she is to others, but who is she to you? Let's give her a name.

An executive coach with whom I have worked for nearly a decade asked me this question a few years back. She invited me to name the various roles I play in my life theater, such as the 'Eye of the Tiger' (the creative, achieving executive), 'Aunt Debbie' (the doting, fun mom named affectionately after one of my aunts), as well as several others that I have waiting in the proverbial wings to usher on stage when appropriate.

The role I crave most, the one who is calling to me from the reflection? She is the one who has achieved an evolved role, carrying me through work, play, motherhood, and the absolute beauty and power of being a woman.

She is flowing, she taps into the beauty around her; she is desired and connected, patient and knowing. She saunters through life with ease – soft and wise, powerful and yielding, maternal and striking. She is a mother, a creator, a source of strength and boundless energy.

She takes care of herself. The maternal role is no longer just for her children, but rather mothering the corners of her own being that crave her attention.

She creates. From the dreamt concept to the written page, or the stage, her creative pathway is clear and charged, allowing for the possible realities to unfold and she to relish in them taking flight.

She is inspired, and when not she puts her feet and her hands in the earth. She is not confined by ideas or ideals, not confined by a past list or any human, or the weather, or the boss, or the bank account. She is a fluid identity that ebbs and flows and may still write things down and check things off but does so at her own will.

"Does this serve me now?" is her question.

She is named the Maternal Earth Goddess.

This goddess isn't new to me. She has shown up in several forms and moments of my life and embodies the best of my moments, the best of my reflection, the best of my pride and joy wrapped up into a wild, curious, gorgeous vision. I adore her, and when I achieve this embodiment, I feel my best, and my life around me syncs.

Who are you, beloved reader, now? Who is that beautiful, knowing woman in the reflection? She is ever evolving, and being all-knowing, she is ready for you. Give her a name. Give her life. Tell her that you've heard her calling, and you are ready to answer.

10
THE INTENTIONAL IDENTITY

How does this named identity – just one of the many roles you play – enable you to flow, create, remain inspired and boundless between 6am and 7pm? All in between awaking from restless slumber, brewing matcha, packing lunches, jumping on calls, building action plans, presenting, pickups, saving lives or saving businesses, drop offs, breathing in fresh air, sharing a bite with your person or children, walking the dog, twice, and your fascia release routine to remove the elevens from your knitted brows?

Ah. Reading that back sounds exhausting.

In fact, if we listed all the planned and random moments of the day it would not only read as 'exhausting' but also impossible.

This is not a hero moment to relish in achieving the impossible. It's an eye-opening realization that too often we live our lives on autopilot – going through motions, without thinking, based on habits and learned defaults.

We have trained our brains to complete tasks in default mode from sun up to sun down, that due to our enterprising and instinctual gifts, may seem on the outside looking in as a success. Autopilot is not confined by the walls of our office or home. It extends to the airport, to the board meeting, to the cocktail party, to scrolling, to the random moments that fill up the spaces in between. We find ourselves begging for rest or being restless in the evening and pop back up after seven hours to operate again. We pride ourselves on being reliable – the go-to leaders, the problem solvers, the ones who never drop the ball. We create an illusion of progress while disconnecting from our personal needs and desires. We rarely ask ourselves if we are aligned with our true aspirations, or even know what they are, and while we defend the 'accomplishments' of the hours spent yesterday or yesteryear, we realize that experiencing true moments of joy and pride and deep connection are few and far between.

We are stuck in a loop of do, reap, rest, do, reap, rest. Let's shed this veil of rigidity and cloak of repetition. Let's stop validating our existence by working hard, as autopilot is the enemy of evolution.

It is time to evolve.

Evolve, not create an escape plan. Rather than feverishly searching your travel apps for flights to satisfy an immediate release of dopamine, let's draw immediate attention to that goddess in the mirror and acknowledge that all she desires is within her, and within reach.

* * *

What do you desire?

Desire is a delicious word that stirs emotion. When was the last time you desired something, or acted on a desire? What of late has your heart raced with excitement?

Your mind will try to answer this question first. It will speak up rather quickly, and be quite practical, and safe, in its response. Or, by default, your mind may mimic something you've seen or been predisposed to by algorithms feeding you imagery. Desire is visceral. Disregard the voice in your head and the constructs of the digital world. Instead, feel where in your body lights up when you think about desire.

The word desire begs me to allow a smile; I feel warmth washing over my body. I imagine sitting cross legged on a board room table, grey pin striped pencil skirt and large gold necklace, a skyline, and a signed book deal.

Or, a candlelit kitchen, Benny Goodman on the Sonos, and my husband and I sitting knee to knee at the counter with a warm homemade meal, whispered conversations and laughter.

So, what do you desire? What stirs inside you that being mindlessly 'busy' you may have ignored or disregarded? Where in your life is this vision targeted – your relationship, your career, your home, your body? Is it something you have suppressed, or forgot about, or is it something new, sparked by the freedom for your authentic self to settle back in and start pitching ideas again?

Desire is a big word. A big emotion. You've just wrestled it out from under the suppressed thumb of the laundry list you've operated under for so long, so allow this once-repressed stirring to overwhelm you for a moment. Capture your desires now, ink them to the page. It isn't carving them in stone; it's a spark of inspiration from the fire set to what no longer serves you.

It's a few seeds of your next era, planted in the embers of the honored yet discarded identity of the past that could yield a wild garden of a more passionate experience ripe for the taking.

A passionate experience requires passion. The word itself feels cinematic, available to us emotionally in brief bouts only after a great film, or book, or experience. We relish it for a moment and then wash our face, tidy up, and rest up for a new day. Our serious breadwinning shell of the past would have weighed the options of passion versus purpose. Why? Because passion requires play, and play may sound frivolous. But it is just a word, and reframing a word can induce an emotion. Emotion inspires action. And action is interesting. So…

Are you the most interesting woman in the room?

* * *

On a recent business trip in Toronto, I was dining alongside six of my new team members, and one gentleman was sharing how he picked up windsurfing a year ago and is now starting his mornings on the West coast in the ocean. Another team member from Boston has a standing Saturday sail with his teenagers. Another living in Toronto plays rugby twice a week in an adult league. All eyes were suddenly on me as I was asked about my hobbies.

I didn't have any to share.

And I was no longer the most interesting woman in the room. Or interesting to myself.

Hobbies are pursuits outside of our careers that we are passionate about. And I could not comprehend where in my day I would have time to spend an hour on something else, let alone several days on end, mastering how to tack or gybe downwind. But when I dove into how I spend my days, it wasn't a lack of time that was the problem. It was my lack of spending my free moments with intention. Instead, due to autopilot, I resort to a 'quick' and mindless scroll, find something to tackle to check a box on my to-do list, or tend to someone else's perceived needs.

Once back in the states, after cringing at myself, I pondered the question my new boss asked me. What are, or would be, my hobbies? What am I actually passionate about?

I love tennis. I was in a league for four years and recently committed to playing on a team again this spring. But I have not prioritized tennis in my free time.

I have a love for physics. Newton's first law is my favorite to recite, committed to memory since the 11th grade. I happen to come across physics professors on my travels and we spend time discussing theories and space while waiting to board flights. But I have not prioritized physics in my free time.

I love art. I love hiking. I love fashion. I love baking. I love writing and reading. But I have not prioritized any of these pursuits in my free time. I've tacked a weekend onto a business trip to Vegas to visit Zion National Park but haven't explored the dozens of hiking trails within 40 minutes from Charleston. I'll load four books on my Kindle and literally take three books out of the actual library, but nine pages get read and the loans lapse.

The majority of my male counterparts are passionate about their hobbies. Fly fishing, skiing, hunting, gardening, chess, surfing, golf, ultra-marathons. My husband will pause work for 30 minutes daily to turn up the amp and play his guitar. They make the time, they schedule the activity, and have the go bag at the ready. They prioritize their passions and even share them with friends. They are interesting.

I want to be interesting, too. First, for my own opinion of myself. Second, to experience more richness, spontaneity, and intention in this season of my life.

And you?

That woman in the mirror – what is she curious about? What interests her? What would she talk about in a circle of peers that engages and begs more detail to be shared? What conversation would she spark with her partner during a free afternoon or weekend morning? What would strengthen her pursuit of excellence?

Here's a jumpstart:

• **Recite and reflect on poetry:** Select a few of the literary greats and scour old bookstores for early editions, perhaps color coordinate a shelf of your finds to inspire reading and memorizing passages that inspire you.

• **Explore state and national parks:** Download the All Trails app, prepare your go bag with all terrain shoes, and immerse yourself in nature. Start local, bring the dog or a friend if you like, and share your findings with peers on the app. Before you know it, you'll be flying to Glacier or Canyonlands to hike Sperry Glacier Trail or The Maze.

• **Join a team, hire a coach/trainer:** Tennis, martial arts, basketball, or any other athletic endeavor. The friendly competition, comradery and discipline of practice not only infuse your spirit but offer lessons transferable to your role as leader and collaborator at work.

• **Investing:** Whether day trading, real estate, or buying 'boring businesses', the capital gains are personal and professional, infusing natural abilities to assess risk and achieve at the same time. Whether just dabbling or en route to be an expert, join a peer group, create one, or dive into podcasts, books, and trading resources.

• **Gardening:** A dear friend of mine was interested in citrus after reading an article, signed up for a citrus class at a local nursery, and is reaping the rewards of fresh, organic lemons and limes in terracotta pots on her patio. This same friend learned of herbal remedies and built and planted an apothecary garden as a source for homemade teas, cleaning products, and nourishment. She is literally reaping the rewards of her labor.

Need more inspiration?

Jot down three ideas that:

1. Move your body

2. Increase knowledge

3. Channel creativity

Inspiration triggers the brain to release positive neurochemicals, enhancing our cognitive state and creating a desire for action. This action could translate to learning new skills, which in turn creates new patterns of stimulation, forming new neural pathways and stimulating neuroplasticity, enhancing brain function and resilience. In a TedX talk given by Dr. Lara Boyd, she notes "Increased difficulty, increased struggle during practice, actually leads to more learning and greater structural change in the brain... Behaviors you employ in your everyday life are important.[4]"

4   After watching this, your brain will not be the same | Lara Boyd | TEDxVancouver

Let's take it a step further by employing a daily behavior such as a 'Closed Laptop Rule.' I mark this point in time daily in my planner with a bold line drawn at a specific time each day, a time that allows for meetings to happen and space to collect thoughts before ending work. Once the laptop is closed it does not get reopened. Work email is not checked on my phone. This is a shutdown.

Consistent access to work allows it to infiltrate any minute or hour of our day. We are subconsciously waiting for the next ping of teams, waiting for the next request, the need for our time and attention. Allowing work at any time will never permit space for creativity, desire, and passion to surface. Instead, it limits the attention span we have for everything else. Have you ever had an idea spark after a lovely family dinner and then rushed to the laptop to try to work it out, only to realize two hours have passed and it's now 10:15PM and the solution has not quite materialized?

Turn instead to post-it-notes.

I have post-it-notes all over our home. In my office, by my nightstand, in my vehicle and in my bag. Go figure, over a cup of matcha in the early hours of the morning, stretched and having meditated, a creative idea for the report I couldn't figure out yesterday pops into my mind. Feverishly I write it down on the post-it-note and leave it be. It is now concrete and available for later. I return to my matcha. When it is time to open my laptop, I then collect and act upon the ideas captured during the time carved out for that specific function.

My husband keeps a notebook by his bedside for just these moments of inspiration. Years ago, he awoke around 3AM with song lyrics in his head and jotted them down, then returned to his slumber. At 6AM he arose, gathered his guitar, a coffee, and the bedside notebook and completed the song 'Chevy '55', a crowd favorite, before 9AM.

Give yourself the space to allow yourself to create with stillness. Whether a two-minute focus on breath between meetings or an early morning meditation on the porch, be intentional no matter how much, or little, time you take to quiet your mind. The moment you do, however, that subconscious taps on your shoulder and begs attention. Ideas will come, but it will start as your to do list. The mind will beg your attention to address tasks – finish folding laundry, your kitchen sink is messy, the flight wasn't booked, the report is due Friday...

Let those pass. Focus on breathing down to the most bottom part of your body that you can reach. Your chest, your belly, your base, your toes. Let your body completely relax. Trust in the comfort of being with just yourself. Without distractions allowed, you will be surprised at what presents itself from a deeper place, limitless and unbound, activating your brain, stimulating growth, rejuvenating your cells.

Stillness and a quiet mind ripe for creation and exploration is the new definition of luxurious freedom. Have your post-it-notes or notebook nearby, as your inspired spirit loves the space to run wild. What will emerge? Clarity and a fresh perspective, intertwined with intention. Combined with our innate capability to pursue what we desire and what inspires us, we become, again, the most intentional, interesting humans to the most important ones of all – ourselves.

11

THE LEGACY

Entering this next biological phase of our lives, physically, emotionally, mentally, and spiritually, is liberating. We have laid the groundwork, and, with our past experiences and 'newfound' wisdom, have a sense of freedom from conforming to what once was, or what was once believed to be true.

This was not the responsibility of our mentors, the mostly men who raised us in corporate America. How could they have anticipated or taught us how to prepare for a female's spirit splitting dilemma? Our mentors took us under their wings and helped us go after what they thought we were after: the original journey to learn, climb, earn, reap the rewards.

Yet we missed the connection of that journey to our deepest, warmest, most feminine space within. This, says my holistic health practitioner here in Charleston[5], who is experienced in bridging the ancient traditions between Western and Eastern medicines, "was divinely designed as a sacred space, a literal and metaphorical container. It's where life begins, yes, but it's also where we hold the echoes of the women who came before us—our mothers, grandmothers, and all their resilience and strength."

The women before us.

I am, we are, the result of generations of women who desired to leave their legacy, to put a stake in the ground, to love and be loved. They were different and differently empowered than we are now. As my holistic practitioner also beautifully stated, "The empowered woman has a legacy of other women that she built upon even though they did it differently and radically; their DNA is the framework that gives the foundation for her root. Think of ourselves as women of the trees, our roots go deep so we can hold our branches and our arms out, and in between is where all of the nourishment is created and held within the womb. From the creation of seed to our daughters in the future and from our grandmothers who are weighted down in their branches by all that they hold. Like trees, we are divinely designed to bend and break and grow – we are always rooted. Our roots never let us fail. When the storm comes, we shake our branches, bathe ourselves in the refreshing rain. Knowing that I have faith, I have destiny, and I am able to move forward even though I am standing still."[1]

5   A. McClam (personal conversation October 3, 2024)

The irony is that I feel such pride and awe reflecting on the lives led by the women in my ancestry yet have neglected to consider how their influence has shaped the roots of who I am today.

Born in 1897, my great grandmother Anna was a suffragette, a working woman who desired her own income, a world traveler, a medical curiosity who was unable to conceive due to a melon sized tumor in her uterus, yet at the age of 35 gave birth to her only child, my maternal grandmother. My great grandmother passed away when I was eight, but I fondly remember her smile, the gentleness of her presence, her meticulous home and gardens, and the way she watched the three generations of humans she had created with admiration.

My paternal grandmother, Barbara, was the offspring of a family of French and English immigrants who fled Europe during the French Revolution and landed in Staten Island, NY. She was a Daughter of the American Revolution, a bubbly, funny, and beautiful woman who skipped school to see Frank Sinatra perform in New York City. She was a working single mother to three in the 1960s after divorcing my grandfather, and, while funny, loving and devoted to her community, I recall a sense of distance and bitterness of not living the life she had desired, a life interrupted by World War II and the loss of true love, unable to fully relinquish the past and be in the present.

My mother is the oldest of five and is the very definition of the word "mother" to her children, her siblings, and all who know her. Growing up in the 60s and 70s, she wore her dirty blonde hair so long it got caught in her belt and was determined to defy the societal norms of being a girl in her era by interviewing to be a gas station attendant, a road construction worker, and a copywriter. She landed two of the three, yet after my father proposed to her in front of the polar bears at The Central Park Zoo and I was born, she wanted only to be a mother. Over the next six years she became a mother to three and once penned the following, "Later, when I am finished turning my angelic-monsters into independent assets to society, then I'll think about what I want to be when I grow up." Yet she also penned this in the late '80s: "Wherever my occupation had to be filled on a form, I couldn't put the word 'Housewife'. It was so degrading. I wanted to put in a title of respect... something that would command more than an eye of nonchalance. More so from the women than the men, I felt this pressure of non-acceptance. I could almost feel them saying I wasn't doing enough. It was about two and a half months into Motherhood that I realized it was Women doing this to Women. I was losing my individuality as a person and worrying too much about what I appeared to be to others. On the space for occupation I put 'Domestic Engineer.' It better described to the world what I really am. This also helped me with the acceptance."

And here we are, too — a bit dissident, torn, proud, rigid, curious, so committed to living a life well lived and being accepted that we cannot seem to shake the weight from our branches. We hold onto it all with a profound desire to showcase our beauty and effort and results of the painstaking pursuit of perfection for those around us and could perhaps be a bit gentler on how we perceive other women and their choices. We are learning, each generation, with those before us sharing their lessons in their unconditional love.

Instead of unbending, unwavering to the outside world, what if we accepted that all we, collectively, need and desire is within us, profoundly impacted by the women that carried us: our mothers and their mothers. Rooted in the fact that we are all already perfectly created with everything we need inside our physical and spiritual bodies – memories, ideas, emotion, intelligence, passion, drive, love. Sit in the acknowledgment of not just those in our present who light the path forward for dreams we set in motion decades ago, but also for those who gave us the life force to be literally, and figuratively here, now.

And as most impeccably stated in 1977, "May the force be with you."

12

THE POWER SOURCE

Armed with desire, inspiration, and intention; gratitude and acknowledgment of our ancestral women; an appreciation for the girl who blazed our life trail with her ambition and big dreams; the emergence of an authentic version of ourselves who is cultivating a new garden of life from the ashes of the original dream burned to the ground, we ask:

How to forge ahead when this life evolution will be just that – continuous creation?

Know that it is fundamentally innate.

Biologically, we as females were literally built to create and sustain life.

This ability is one of the most coveted, dissected, discussed, misconstrued, and mysterious powers of all time – and whether we as women literally or figuratively choose to behold it – we will be criticized for how, when, where, why, and with whom. By both men and women. But we cannot dismiss it.

It is also a power source. And we, as its rightful and majestic owners, are responsible for the care, nurture, and wielding of it.

Yet, we often neglect, or have been conditioned to neglect, this power, whether influenced by others or self-induced suppression, pushed aside to let more masculine energy take control.

Our masculine energy serves its purpose when necessary, yet haven't we come to realize how few and far between the moments are that we need it? Tossing this energy around without consideration and purpose can do more damage than good. Often misunderstood by the beholder, this masculine energy can come across as unauthentic, leaving our audience, and ourselves, both confused and dissident.

Tapping into our feminine power is more diverse and all-capable, allowing a natural ability to flex and flow, command and whisper, manifest and empower, love and be loved – as a leader, as a partner, as a mother, as a contributor, and as a woman who is deeply in love with herself.

This sounds fluffy. And to the serious, ambitious, success-driven woman, this may feel futile and unnecessary, thinking 'I don't have time for this.' 'How do I tap into 'power'? 'Why would I change after accomplishing so much?'

Because our lives depend on it. A life free of pain and rigidity, full of passion and curiosity, and most importantly, a life well lived – true to whoever and whatever we desire to be, have, accomplish, and experience.

This power source resides in our sacral chakra, the second in the system of seven major chakras, that literally holds the power to create life. To behold this power and shoot it up through our being and into the universe, we cannot simply meditate and dream and write and love and sit and magically wait for the world around us to be aligned to our personal and professional calling.

We must first feel safe and held. The root chakra, the first of the major chakras is at the very base of our torso, and while considered a more masculine chakra, is a safety net connected to the physical world associated with the primal energy of survival as well as stability and connection. Our root chakra holds the key to self-worth, self-preservation, and ultimate purpose. Women tend to hold stress, frustration at our base, at our root. Physically, our root chakra relates to cortisol, the stress hormone. And as overachievers, it ignites more 'doing' to satisfy our longing for 'real purpose', ignoring our basic human needs to feel safe and loved.

We do not permit ourselves to be held very often, do we? What if we enabled this sense of safety to not just the base of our physical body but also to those who love us unconditionally?

When was the last time you allowed yourself to be held by another – your partner, your parent, your friend – to be wrapped in their arms, in THEIR intention to just hold you close while you unconditionally accept their love? Allowing your edges to soften, to feel acquiescent for just a moment, to be nothing else to anyone, but loved. Loved and safe. When we feel safe and connected, the flow from our root is sparked to connect to the delicious, divine sacral chakra. When open and flowing, our sacral space creates inspiration, drive, passion, and pleasure. When emitted into the ether, we, too, are desired. Being desired creates attraction which commands action. Permit your whole self to be desired and note the change in your energy, and the energy around you.

* * *

In this practice of allowing myself to be held, figuratively and literally, I have opened a door of creativity that has been only just slightly ajar for such a long time. In my past, I have forced it open, and in moments of complete quiet or meditation it has sparked small fires that I stoked ferociously to capture the inspiration. Instead of using force, I now simply understand that I am. We are, and that is all that is certain. Release the identity and the imbalance that had suited us for some time, release the need to be right, release the need to be everything at once. As powerful, creative, inspiring women let's embrace and acknowledge what we have created and the potential of what is to be created. Let's embrace a vision of ourselves that feels good now.

SO- what feels good now?

We are women, mothers, partners, leaders, creators, maternal earth goddesses. It's time to draft a new list. And this time, revisit it often.

With your pen, or pencil, or keyboard, freely express what you want right now. All of it.

Not as inspiration, but as a sample set. Here is my latest list as I pen this book:

I WANT

- I want to be in charge of my future.
- I want to transition our home with my hands (and contractors!) to fit our life now.
- I want to be on the water with my favorite people often.
- I want to launch my books and speak about women owning their next stage of life basking in success while curating the next experience.
- I want a life concierge.
- I want to work with strong, smart women in pursuit of the wellbeing of others.
- I want to go to the beautiful yoga studio whenever I want.
- I want to schedule and keep appointments for a facial and massage quarterly.
- I want to visit Europe every year or more.
- I want to hike every National Park.
- I want lobster rolls and a house in Maine.
- I want to cold plunge and sauna and drink iced matcha homemade.
- I want to brainstorm and write and strategize with smart people.
- I want to collaborate with scientists, doctors, and physicists on wellbeing.
- I want to want new things and explore.
- I want to be so passionately in love that my eyes tear up.
- I want my children to have zero college/secondary school debt.
- I want my grandchildren to have a pool and a boat and a beach to visit.
- I want to feel overflowing with peace and love.

What is so beautiful is that yours will be different. Yours will feel juicy and delicious to you, and revisiting it often, writing it often, sparks ideas from that day, that time, that moment and permits the crossing off of what does not suit you in that time and space. It's okay to not be so rigid in your wants, and it's okay that a few milestones have dropped off.

I realize that I have not penned 'Earn $X' on this list, and that the law degree hasn't made its comeback. But I have also realized that I am dreaming more of who I will be when my children grow up, what my evolving corporate passions look like, and how I want to feel with my life partner. The list is not too soft; rather, it's dreamy. It's the list of a goddess who feels so grateful for the pursuits of the girl she was.

I say to her, and to you, 'You did good, girl. You did good.' And now, we root up, tap in, and flow for this leg of the journey.

Because all we know for certain is 'I am.'

I am a collection of my past pursuits.

I have a vision of my future.
I am all I need to be.
I have all I need within.

I will honor my spirit and let her guide me.

I cherish my past.

I embrace my present.

and I knowingly create my future.

13

THE BEGINNING

The immensity of this life deserves not just undivided attention but relishing in fulfillment. Leave no path unwandered, no laughter suppressed, no gift not given, no door not knocked upon and no dream put on pause. Let us not regret inaction, but rather go forth in pursuit of our unique evolution.

Burn the success list.

Hug your babies.

Say I love you.

Keep your phone away from your bedside.

Stretch.

Hydrate.

Move your body.

Show kindness.

Plan ahead.

Be spontaneous.

Admire nature.

Wield your power with passion.

Read.

Book the flight.

Launch the idea.

Lend a hand.

Stay in.

Go out.

Leave your desk uncluttered.

Hire someone if you need to.

Get the blowout.

Be barefoot on the lawn.

Say yes to something else, often.

And be flexible when your pursuits change, again.

Let's invite one another to inspire ourselves while creating space for those up next to get the gist a bit earlier in life.

We are so profoundly capable, perfectly put on this earth as a complete package of goddess goodness. Fall in love with your wondrous self over and over again, fill her up with what she needs and desires.

Having it all is simply a personal memory bank of pride and joy, a life of experiences that opens your eyes, mind, and heart.

You've got it from here.

About the Author

Author of "Burn the Success List", National Football League alumni, College of Charleston Executive MBA Program Mentor and senior marketing leader, Jamessina is on a mission to reignite passion and desire in the lives of overachieving, corporate women so they can fall back in love with the life they are creating despite feeling burnt out and on autopilot.

Jamessina is a mother, a marketing leader, mentor, speaker, author and former board member of both Big Brothers Big Sisters of Long Island and Big Brothers Big Sisters of the Lowcountry. Since 2017, Jamessina has guest lectured and served as an executive mentor for the College of Charleston Executive MBA program. She has also led an annual session entitled 'Own Your Power' with the Women of Impact Program at the College of Charleston, focused on navigating corporate America as a multi-faceted woman, leading with strength, empathy, poise and feminine power from within. Having started her career as the first intern for the NFL Youth Football Department, Jamessina's day job for the past decade has been leading demand generation and alliance teams in the enterprise technology industry. She resides in Charleston, SC with her husband and their two children.

For more resources from Jamessina visit burnthesuccesslist.com.

www.ingramcontent.com/pod-product-compliance
Lightning Source LLC
Chambersburg PA
CBHW051532120626
46551CB00012B/1192